HEN KAI PAN

TITAN COMICS
GROUP EDITOR / Jake Devine
DESIGNER / Donna Askem
ASSISTANT EDITOR / Calum Collins
EDITOR / Phoebe Hedges
PRODUCTION CONTROLLERS / Caterina Falqui & Kelly Fenlon
PRODUCTION MANAGER / Jackie Flook
ART DIRECTOR / Oz Browne
SALES & CIRCULATION MANAGER / Steve Tothill
MARKETING COORDINATOR/ Lauren Noding
PUBLICIST / Phoebe Trillo
DIGITAL & MARKETING MANAGER / Jo Teather
HEAD OF RIGHTS / Jenny Boyce
ACQUISITIONS EDITOR / Duncan Baizley
PUBLISHING DIRECTOR / Ricky Claydon
PUBLISHING DIRECTOR / John Dziewiatkowski
OPERATIONS DIRECTOR / Leigh Baulch
PUBLISHERS / Vivian Cheung & Nick Landau

HEN KAI PAN
© 2022 Eldo Yoshimizu. All rights reserved.

This translation first published in 2022 by Titan Comics, a division of Titan Publishing Group, Ltd,
144 Southwark Street, London SE1 0UP, UK.
Titan Comics is a registered trademark of Titan Publishing Group Ltd.

No part of this publication may be reproduced, stored in a retrieval system, or transmitted, in any form or by any means, without the prior written permission of the publisher. Names, characters, places and incidents featured in this publication are either the product of the author's imagination or used fictitiously. Any resemblance to actual persons, living or dead (except for satirical purposes), is entirely coincidental.

10 9 8 7 6 5 4 3 2 1

First edition: April 2022
Printed in India
ISBN: 9781787738379

A CIP catalogue record for this title is available from the British Library.

Hen Kai Pan

WRITER & ARTIST
Eldo Yoshimizu

TRANSLATOR
Matoko Tamamuro

LETTERER
Lauren Bowes

FOREWORD

"The Earth is not just for humankind."

We only hear issues such as climate change, food crises and deforestation being discussed from a human perspective, but suppose the Earth itself had its own thoughts on these matters. How would it feel or react?

This was my starting point for telling this story, so I began work on Hen Kai Pan.

Then Covid-19 struck...

I considered whether now was the right time to be writing a book about the end of human civilisation, when a lot of people were dying and suffering for real.

So, I took a walk in the nearby forest and thought about it.

The plants looked fine.

The birds looked fine.

And I noticed all of this because the factories and other facilities had stopped working, and the traffic volume had decreased.

I noticed the silence.

Wouldn't the Earth be healthier and more energetic without humans, I thought?

I resumed writing Hen Kai Pan.

Sometimes thinking from a different perspective is very important.

Eldo Yoshimizu
Chigasaki, 2021

CHAPTER 1: SPIRITS OF EARTH

WHAT THE HELL!
FIGHT! FUKUSHIMA
がんばろう！福島

WE'VE JUST RECEIVED NEWS FOLLOWING YESTERDAY'S TRANSPORT PLANE CRASH NEAR FUKUSHIMA DAIICHI NUCLEAR POWER STATION IN JAPAN!
THE PLANE INVOLVED WAS FEX167 FLYING FROM KANSAI INTERNATIONAL AIRPORT TO MEMPHIS INTERNATIONAL AIRPORT, U.S.A.

ACCORDING TO EYEWITNESSES, A LARGE PLANE AT AN EXTREMELY LOW ALTITUDE CRASHED INTO THE SEA AFTER SWERVING TO AVOID A COLLISION WITH THE POWER STATION.

THE JAPANESE GOVERNMENT HAS SET UP AN EMERGENCY INQUIRY HEADQUARTERS. IT HAS ANNOUNCED IT WILL LOOK AT THE POSSIBILITY OF IT BEING BOTH TERRORISM AND ACCIDENTAL.

LADAKH, NORTH INDIA

THAT WAS CLOSE.
IT JANGLES THE NERVES...
SHA
SHA

BANGKOK, THAILAND
PAAN
PAN
BEEP

NILA, YOU ARE DOING IT WRONG.

YOU FAILED, DIDN'T YOU? ASURA...
ASURA, A DISCIPLE...YET YOU ARE A WARRIOR WHO WENT THROUGH THE STRICT ASCETICISM...

PLOP
チャプ
PLOP
チャプ
YES...
GO TO AFRICA. I WILL GIVE YOU YOUR NEXT INSTRUCTIONS.
YES, MISS NILA...

MADAGASCAR, AFRICA

ROAAAAR

MISS NILA, I'M ABOVE THE FOREST.
THEN START,
ASURA, WHAT YOU NEED TO DO.

ZUMB

THAT'S WHERE WE PLANTED SAPLINGS LAST YEAR!
WHAT IS THAT BLAST? HAS A WAR BROKEN OUT?

SCREEE
MISS NILA... WHY DID YOU...
...MAKE ME BURN THE FOREST?
FOOLISH HUMANS BURN FORESTS. SO WE DO IT SOME MORE, TO TEACH THEM OF THEIR FOLLY.
SHOW ME THE BLAZING FOREST, THE BEAUTIFUL FLAMES...

AAAAGH!
SQUEAL

SQUEAL
!!

SOMETHING'S COMING! ANIMALS AND BIRDS...AND A HUMAN?

MY NAME IS OMBIASA.
ASURA... WHY ARE YOU DOING THIS?
TO ADD FUEL TO HUMANS' EVIL-DOING. JUST AS I DO NOW.
THAT IS NILA TALKING.
BUT WHAT DO YOU THINK, ASURA?
CLACK
THIS IS GREAT NILA'S ORDER! YOU GOT A FUCKING PROBLEM?

SUCH A THING MEANS NOTHING TO ME. BY THE WAY, THERE IS A PLACE I WOULD LIKE TO SHOW YOU.
YOU WANNA MAKE ME MAD!?
POOR YOU.
ASURA, YOU ARE...
YOU ARE NOTHING BUT NILA'S TOOL.
WHAT A JERK.
THIS WAY. COME.

?
WHAT ARE YOU DOING?
ACCORDING TO THE FOLKLORE AROUND THESE PARTS...
...IT RAINS WHEN A BAOBAB TREE CRIES.

IT'S A DRY SEASON.
THERE'S NO WAY IT WILL RAIN!
RIDICULOUS...
SPLASH

W-WHAT THE...?
THE FOREST FIRE WILL BE EXTINGUISHED.
ASURA!

YOU FAILED AGAIN! YOU CANNOT EVEN DO A SIMPLE THING.
FAILING ONCE IS OKAY, BUT TWICE? WORDS FAIL ME.
SORRY...
SORRY...
AT LEAST LEARN YOUR FOOLISHNESS IN THE RAIN! YOU GOOD-FOR-NOTHING!
SOB...
FORGET WHAT NILA SAID. ASURA, WHY DON'T YOU LISTEN TO THIS TREE'S VOICE?
THE TREE'S VOICE?
ASURA!
ASURA!

ASURA! THAT MAN IS DANGEROUS!
THIS TREE IS BIG AND BIG-HEARTED, TOO.
THE TREE'S ANGRY ABOUT WHAT I'VE DONE, RIGHT?
COME ON.
ASURA! NO!
ASURA! WHAT ARE YOU DOING? STOP IT!
WILL YOU DISOBEY ME?
I'LL CUT OFF TELEPATHIC COMMUNICATION JUST FOR A SHORT WHILE.
...SORRY MISS NILA...

VSSSHHH
I CAN'T HEAR ANYTHING!
VSSSHHH
ASURA, THAT IS BECAUSE YOUR HEART IS LOCKED.
OPEN YOUR HEART AND HUG THE TREE.
VSSSHHH
VSSSHHH
HUH!

MISTRESS PEMAJUNGNE!
THIS IS PEMAJUNGNE.
I AM TALKING TO YOU THROUGH THIS TREE.
YOU ARE ASURA, NILA'S DISCIPLE, AREN'T YOU?

YOU KNOW OF THE JUDGMENT DAY WHEN WE, THE SPIRITS OF EARTH, WILL JUDGE HUMANITY.

I WILL MAKE THE FINAL JUDGMENT AFTER ASKING THOUGHTS AND OPINIONS FROM THE FOUR SPIRITS.

HOWEVER, NILA...

...HAS ARBITRARILY STARTED THE JUDGMENT EARLY. USING YOU...

!!

YOU ARE NOT NILA'S TOOL.

I DO NOT WISH YOU TO COMMIT ANY MORE CRIMES.

NILA'S METHOD WILL DESTROY NOT ONLY HUMANITY, BUT ALSO THE EARTH'S ECOSYSTEM.

THAT WOULD BRING AN END TO THE WORLD.

CHAPTER 2:
A FLAME OF ICE

LOIRE REGION,
FRANCE

ASURA THE DISCIPLE... I CAN SENSE AN AGITATION IN YOUR QI.
I-I AM FINE, MISS NILA!
PEMAJUNGNE HAS BEEN PUTTING IDEAS IN YOUR HEAD.
NO! THAT'S NOT TRUE!

THE IDEAS OF MISTRESS PEMAJUNGNE AND OTHERS ARE TOO SOFT FOR HUMANS. BELIEVE ME.

YOU WILL BE THE SPIRIT OF WAR.

YES... MISS NILA...

THE ARCTIC CIRCLE, OFF THE COAST OF SVALBARD.
I HAVE ARRIVED AT THE PLACE. MISS NILA... WHAT SHOULD I DO HERE...?
THE TARGET WILL BE RIGHT UNDERNEATH YOU.
HUH...? RIGHT UNDERNEATH HERE...?
GET OFF THE SNOWMOBILE. KNEEL ON THE ICE.

YES... MISS NILA...
US NAVY VIRGINIA-CLASS NUCLEAR-POWERED SUBMARINE

BOTH HANDS ON ICE.
...YES...
I CAN STILL DETECT A SLIGHT AGITATION IN YOUR QI. PULL YOURSELF TOGETHER.
I-I'M SORRY MISS NILA! I'LL CONCENTRATE.
I SHALL WITHDRAW YOUR INTRINSIC POWER...
Y-YES!
IN THE DARK SEA SEALED BY ICE...LET US LIGHT AN ETERNAL FLAME.
!
JOLT

BANG
WHAT'S THAT?
NOTHING ON THE SONAR OR THE RADAR! NO SHIPS AROUND HERE! NO CONTACTS!
ALL HANDS, BATTLE STATIONS!
ENGINE ROOM HERE! REACTOR CORE TEMPERATURE IS GOING THROUGH THE ROOF!
WHAT THE FUCK?
CALM DOWN! ALL SECTIONS RUN DIAGNOSTICS!
WHRRRR
INSERT THE CONTROL RODS! CHECK THE CORE TEMPERATURE EVERY TWENTY SECONDS!

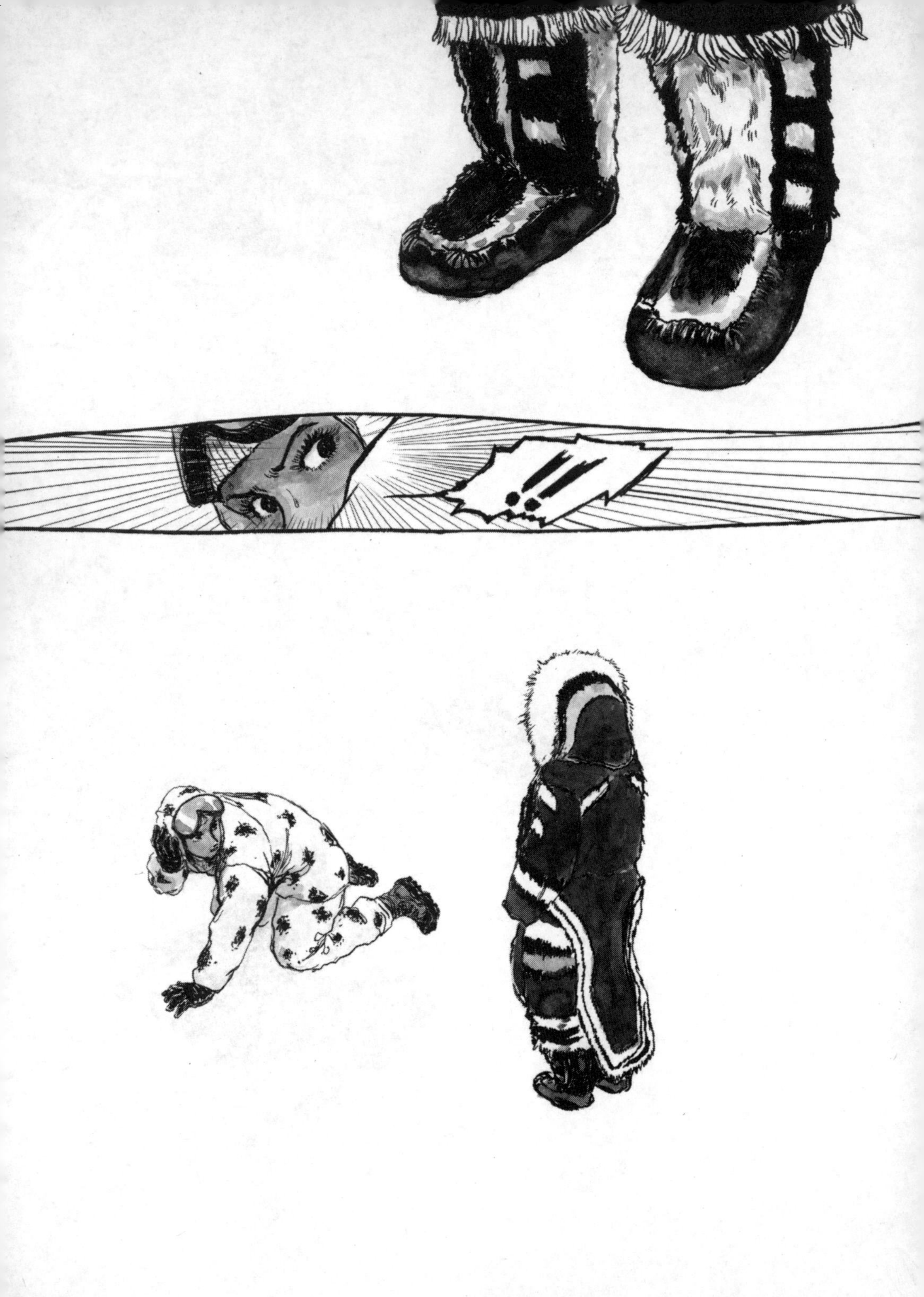

UGH!
!?

STOP IT!
YOU'RE THE SPIRIT OF WAR, YET ARE YOU AFRAID TO DIE?
NATURALLY!
BANG
DIE ONCE, AND YOU'LL SEE.

CAPTAIN! I HEARD WHAT SOUNDS LIKE A GUNSHOT! ON THE ICE RIGHT ABOVE THIS SHIP!
A GUNSHOT?
REACTOR TEMPERATURE IS DROPPING.
OOOOOOHHHH!!!!!
HOW THICK IS THE ICE?
APPROXIMATELY ONE METER!
ALL RIGHT, TAKE US UP!
SURFACE! MAIN BALLAST BLOW! PREPARE FOR IMPACT!
WHRRRR

CAN YOU SEE ANYTHING?
THUMP
NOTHING WITHIN THREE CLICKS. NO REACTION ON THE THERMAL RADAR!
I MUST'VE MISHEARD THE GUNSHOT...

ASURA!
ASURA!

ASURA!
ASURA!

WHERE ARE WE?
IS THIS THE WORLD BEYOND DEATH?
YOU WON'T DIE.
OR RATHER, YOU CAN'T DIE.
CAN'T DIE...?
WHO ARE YOU?
I'M XU FU.
HOW ARE YOU? HAVING DIED ONCE?

I HOPE YOU ARE GRATEFUL. I HAVE RELEASED YOU FROM NILA'S SPELL.
HUH? SPELL?
IT MEANS YOU'RE NO LONGER NILA'S TOOL.
BUT YOU ARE STILL IMMATURE...
TO GROW TO BE A TRUE SPIRIT, THINK FOR YOURSELF. ACT UPON YOUR OWN WILL.
USE YOUR LITTLE BRAIN TO THE FULL AND THINK.
XU FU...WHAT D'YOU THINK ABOUT THE JUDGMENT?

MY OPINION?
I THINK IT'S BETTER TO ERASE HUMANITY.
LOOK. NORTHERN LIGHTS.
ERASE...?

THIS PLANET
IS BEAUTIFUL.

CHAPTER 3: CONFLICT

IT'S HOT... XU FU, WHY ARE WE IN A DESERT?
STOP WHINING! THERE IS ANOTHER SPIRIT HERE FOR YOU TO MEET.

XU FU...
WHY ON EARTH ARE YOU...IN THAT FORM?
WELL...
SOUTHERN ARIZONA, UNITED STATES OF AMERICA
ZERO POINT
HONGA! SORRY TO KEEP YOU WAITING!
HUH? WHAT'RE YOU DOING?
YOU SHOULD GET HUMANS TO PICK UP WHAT THEY'VE THROWN AWAY.

TRAVEL CAUTION
SMUGGLING AND ILLEGAL IMMIGRATION MAY BE ENCOUNTERED IN THIS AREA
AS YOU CAN SEE, RUBBISH PICKING.
YOU'RE HERE.
THIS IS MY JOB. I'M LIVING AS A HUMAN.

I'M HONGA. NICE TO MEET YA!
THIS IS ASURA.
NILA'S DISCIPLE AND TRAINEE.
HIYA.
IF YOU'RE TRAINING TO BE THE SPIRIT OF WAR, YOU'VE GOT STAMINA, HUH? GIMME A HAND.
TAKE THIS TRASH TO MY TRUCK.
O-OKAY...
SEE YA, ASURA! I'LL GO HOME AFTER GETTING SOME MINOR BUSINESS DONE.
AT THE TIME OF THE JUDGMENT... I'M COUNTING ON YOU, LADY ASURA.
HEY! XU FU!

COUNTING ON ME?
WHAT'RE YOU MAKING ME DO? TRASH PICKING, HUH?
STOP SHOUTING. COME NOW.
SHIT!

!
MISTRESS PEMAJUNGNE...
GOOD EVENING, NILA.
AS JUDGEMENT DAY IS DRAWING NEAR...
I WOULD LIKE TO TALK WITH YOU ONE MORE TIME.
VROOOOM
GEEZ. THANKS TO YOU, I MADE PROGRESS.
NO PROBLEM...
WHAT'S THAT?

A HUMAN INVENTION CALLED A BORDER WALL.
VROOOOM
SCREECH
STOP!
WHAT'S THE MATTER?
THE PRESIDENT HAS COME TO INSPECT THE WALL. WE MUST ASK YOU TO MAKE A DETOUR.
POLICE
BORDER PATROL
!!

DAMN, IT'S A DEER... IT MADE ME JUMP.
OH, THAT'S NOT A DEER BUT A PRONGHORN. A SONORAN PRONGHORN THAT LIVES AROUND HERE.
BUT...THAT HEIGHT...HOW DID IT GET THERE?
!?
!!
MR P-PRESIDENT! WE'RE...ON THE M-MEXICAN SIDE!
EMERGENCY! THE PRESIDENT AND MAYOR HAVE DISAPPEARED!
WHAT THE HELL

EMERGENCY! GO GO GO!
VROOOOM
BORDER PATROL
I WONDER WHAT HAPPENED.
XU FU MUST'VE DONE SOMETHING.
XU FU...?
THE SONORAN PRONGHORNS XU FU TOOK OVER HAVE BEEN LIVING ON THIS CONTINENT FOR TEN THOUSAND YEARS.
HUMANS HAVE HUNTED THEM ALMOST TO EXTINCTION. THEN, THAT WALL CUT THEIR REMAINING HABITAT IN TWO.
HE'S BEEN SAYING HUMANS SHOULD BE EXTINCT.
PERHAPS THAT'S WHY HE HATES HUMANS.

HONGA, MAY I ASK YOU SOMETHING?
VROOOM
WHAT?
YOU'VE TOLD MISTRESS PEMAJUNGNE YOUR OPINION, RIGHT?
HONGA... WHAT IS YOUR OPINION ABOUT HUMANS?
I RECKON THEIR BIGGEST PROBLEM IS... CONFLICTS WITH EACH OTHER.
CONFLICTS...
BUT... OTHER ANIMALS... EVEN BIRDS AND FISH FIGHT FOR TERRITORY.
SURE. ANIMALS KILL FOR FUN, TOO.
BUT THE SIZE OF HUMAN CONFLICTS HAS BECOME TOO BIG. NOTHING LIKE THOSE OF ANIMALS.
WHEN HUMANS FIGHT, OTHER CREATURES GET CAUGHT UP IN IT. AND IT DAMAGES THE EARTH.

WHERE ARE WE?

A HOPI RESERVATION.

MISTRESS PEMAJUNGNE IS PROBABLY WEIGHING ALL OUR IDEAS NOW-- NILA'S, OMBIASA'S, XU FU'S, AND MINE.

I'M SENDING A MESSAGE FROM HERE FOR THE JUDGMENT.
THAT BIRD... COMING THIS WAY...
IT'S NILA'S VOTE THAT WORRIES ME.

HONGA! THIS IS PEMAJUNGNE.
MISTRESS PEMAJUNGNE? WHAT'S UP?
NILA REFUSED TO JUDGE WITH US...
SHE WILL CARRY OUT HER OWN JUDGMENT ALONE.
WHAT IS SHE GOING TO DO?
SHE WILL PERHAPS...REVERSE THE EARTH'S GEOMAGNETIC POLES.
WHAT? IF SO... THE WHOLE EARTH WILL BE...!

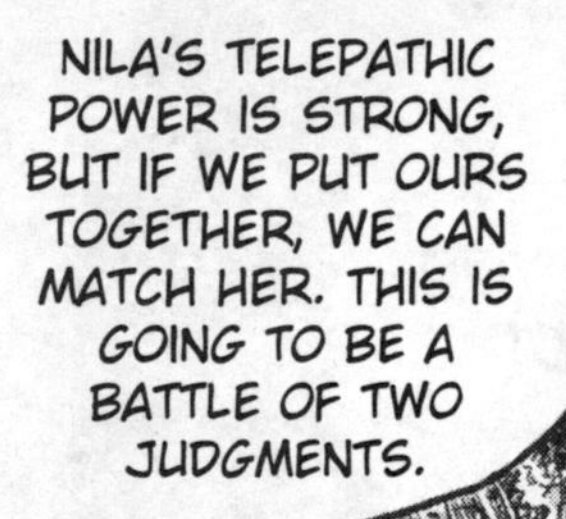
I WILL TRY TO PERSUADE HER ONE LAST TIME. IF THAT FAILS, THEN WE HAVEN'T GOT A CHOICE... EXCEPT TO SEAL NILA'S POWER.
NILA'S TELEPATHIC POWER IS STRONG, BUT IF WE PUT OURS TOGETHER, WE CAN MATCH HER. THIS IS GOING TO BE A BATTLE OF TWO JUDGMENTS.
MISTRESS PEMAJUNGNE... WHAT SHOULD I...?
WHEN SENDING TELEPATHY, HONGA, XU FU, AND OMBIASA WILL BECOME VULNERABLE.
ASURA, I WOULD LIKE YOU TO...PROTECT ALL THREE.
HONGA, I SHALL TRY TO PERSUADE HER FOR THE LAST TIME.
TAKE CARE, MISTRESS PEMAJUNGNE.

ASURA, I WOULD LIKE YOU TO...PROTECT ALL THREE.
IF YOU SUPPORT NILA'S IDEA, FORGET WHAT I SAID.
YOU ARE FREE. ACT ACCORDING TO YOUR OWN WILL.
LASTLY, I TELL YOU THIS. I WILL ERADICATE HUMANITY, BUT I WON'T KILL LIFE.
BECAUSE...
ALL LIFE FORMS ARE DIVINE.

MY OWN WILL...
SHE'LL ERADICATE BUT NOT KILL? DOESN'T MAKE SENSE...ALSO... HOW CAN I PROTECT THE THREE IN SEPARATE LOCATIONS AT THE SAME TIME...?

CHAPTER 4: MISTRESS AND DISCIPLE

NILA...

WHY ARE YOU MAKING ASURA DO THAT?

OH...THAT IS BECAUSE ASURA IS GOING TO BE THE SPIRIT OF WAR. SHE SHINES THE MOST WHEN SHE SLAUGHTERS AND VIOLATES.

ASURA IS A GOD OF DESTRUCTION, MISTRESS PEMAJUNGNE...

SURE...FOR GOOD OR BAD ASURA IS A GOD OF DESTRUCTION...
BUT THE POWER SHOULD BE HERS TO USE. IT IS WRONG FOR YOU TO CONTROL THAT.

HUH!
ASURA IS STILL A CHILD. I MUST GUIDE HER.

MISTRESS PEMAJUNGNE... DID YOU SUMMON ME TO TALK ABOUT ASURA?
NO. NILA...I WOULD LIKE YOU TO JOIN THE JUDGMENT... MY JUDGMENT IS CLEAR.
LEAVE ME ALONE! I HAVE TOLD YOU MANY TIMES! I WILL MAKE MY OWN JUDGMENT!
...I SEE... SHAME...
I HAVE A DUTY TO RESPECT YOUR OPINION, TOO. BUT COULD YOU TELL ME WHICH WAY YOU ARE LEANING?

HUMANITY IS A CANCER ON THE FACE OF THE EARTH.

IT HAS TO BE CUT OUT. OTHERWISE, IT WILL EAT THE EARTH AWAY.

MY JUDGMENT IS CLEAR.
I WILL RESET EARTH IN ORDER TO SAVE IT.
IT IS NO GOOD ERADICATING HUMANITY ALONE. THIS REQUIRES A DRASTIC REMEDY. EVERYTHING FROM THE SKY, THE SEA AND THE LAND.
EVEN CATTLE AND PETS. EVERYTHING THE POISON HAS TOUCHED. THAT'S WHY I WILL REVERSE THE POLARITY OF THE WORLD.
I SEE. NOW I UNDERSTAND YOUR THOUGHTS. I SHARE SOME OF YOUR SENTIMENTS...
BUT, A GEOMAGNETIC REVERSAL WOULD DESTROY EARTH ITSELF.

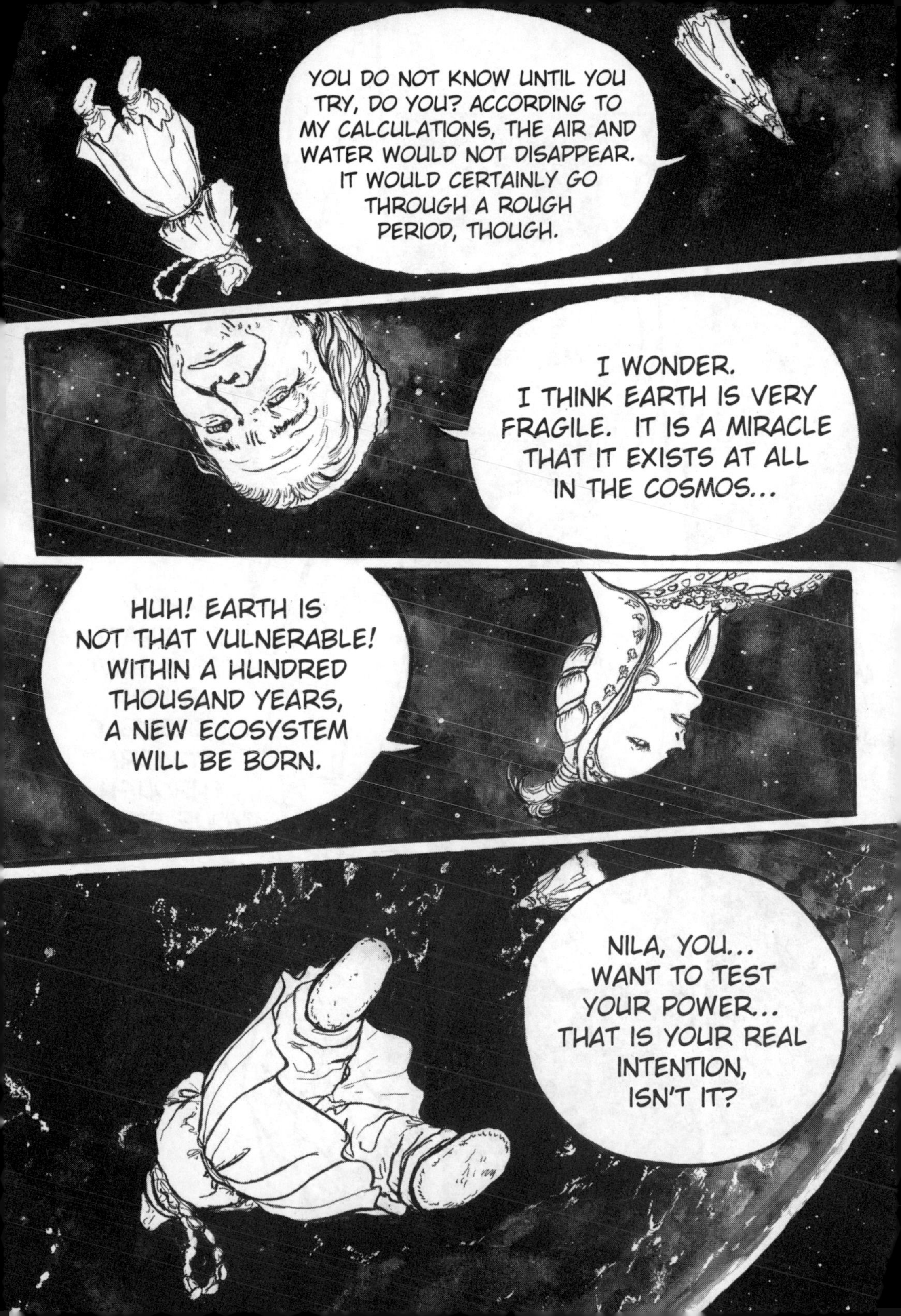

YOU DO NOT KNOW UNTIL YOU TRY, DO YOU? ACCORDING TO MY CALCULATIONS, THE AIR AND WATER WOULD NOT DISAPPEAR. IT WOULD CERTAINLY GO THROUGH A ROUGH PERIOD, THOUGH.
I WONDER. I THINK EARTH IS VERY FRAGILE. IT IS A MIRACLE THAT IT EXISTS AT ALL IN THE COSMOS...
HUH! EARTH IS NOT THAT VULNERABLE! WITHIN A HUNDRED THOUSAND YEARS, A NEW ECOSYSTEM WILL BE BORN.
NILA, YOU... WANT TO TEST YOUR POWER... THAT IS YOUR REAL INTENTION, ISN'T IT?

HAHAHA! SO WHAT? YES, I HAVE GAINED INCREDIBLE POWER! THROUGH YOUR STRICT ASCETIC PRACTICES... MY POWER NOW IS STRONGER THAN YOURS!

YES...IT MAY BE.

MISTRESS! TELL ME YOUR JUDGMENT.

I WILL PUNISH HUMANITY.

I WILL KILL HUMAN CIVILIZATION. I WILL KILL HUMAN BODIES. BUT...

I WILL NOT KILL LIFE.

...SUCH DIFFICULT JUDGMENT...EVEN FOR YOU, IT IS IMPOSSIBLE.
YOU ARE RIGHT. I CANNOT DO IT ON MY OWN. SO...
...I WILL HAVE HELP FROM OTHER SPIRITS.

OTHER SPIRITS...
XU FU... HONGA...
MISTRESS PEMAJUNGNE! MISTRESS!
FAREWELL, NILA...
OMBIASA...
YOU MEAN... ASURA, TOO?
NO USE GATHERING POWER FROM INEPT SPIRITS!
YOU ARE NO MATCH FOR MY POWER...
I WILL WIN!

OMBIASA! CAN YOU HEAR ME?

YES, MISTRESS PEMAJUNGNE. I AM HEADING TO THE PLACE OF MEDITATION TO SEND MY THOUGHTS.

XU FU! THE JUDGMENT WILL START SOON. STAY ALERT!

NILA WILL TRY
TO DISRUPT YOU.
BE CAREFUL!

I CAN FEEL NILA'S STRONG MALICE. NOW... IT ALL DEPENDS ON... ASURA.

SEEMS TO HAVE STARTED...
NOW I SHALL START MY JUDGMENT, TOO...

MISTRESS PEMAJUNGNE...
I AM DIFFERENT FROM WHEN I WAS YOUR DISCIPLE.
MY POWER IS GREAT...

RUMBLE RUMBLE
WE SHALL BEGIN, OMBIASA!
WELL... THERE IS A PROBLEM...
THE LOCAL ARMY HAS TURNED UP. THEY RARELY COME TO THIS FOREST...
SEEMS LIKE THEY ARE LOOKING FOR ME...
I AM SURE NILA IS CONTROLLING THEM! MOVE TO A DIFFERENT PLACE WITHOUT BEING SEEN! TAKE CARE!

ヒュウウウウウウ
WHOOOSH
XU FU!
XU FU! ARE YOU ALL RIGHT THERE?
NOT ALL RIGHT AT ALL! NILA'S GONNA SERIOUSLY KILL US!

HONGA! TELL ME! I MIGHT BE ABLE TO PROTECT YOU!
BUT! HOW CAN I PROTECT XU FU AND OMBIASA FROM AFAR? AND AT THE SAME TIME! THERE'S NO WAY.
YOU HAVE THE POWER TO DO THAT. YOU DIED ONCE, RIGHT? AT THAT TIME YOUR POWER MUST'VE BEEN RELEASED.
MUST'VE BEEN...YOU SAID...BUT I DON'T FEEL ANY DIFFERENT!

RUMBLE RUMBLE

SOMETHING'S COMING!
SOLDIERS, I SEE...AS EXPECTED, MISS NILA HAS...
!
HONGA! THEY'RE SHOOTING. GET DOWN!
RUMBLE RUMBLE

DOWN, HONGA...!
THE JUDGMENT HAS STARTED...

CHAPTER 5: AWAKENING

DOOM

ZHUBABABA
WOW!
ASURA!
!!

ASURA! WHAT ON EARTH ARE YOU DOING?
YOU ARE MY DISCIPLE! DO YOU FORGET YOU ARE MY SERVANT?

...MISS NILA... I'M SORRY...
ASURA...
YOU ARE MERELY BEWITCHED BY MISTRESS PEMAJUNGNE. WAKE UP.
NO...THIS IS WHAT I...DECIDED ON MY OWN.
BOY! YOU HAVE BECOME IMPERTINENT...
THEN I ASK YOU! DO YOU THINK MY JUDGMENT IS WRONG?
I DON'T KNOW.
I DON'T KNOW IF MISTRESS PEMAJUNGNE IS REALLY CORRECT, EITHER.

ASURA... YOU ARE STILL IN TWO MINDS EVEN NOW...

YOU ARE NOT EVEN FIT TO BE THE SPIRIT OF WAR. THE POWERFUL WOULD NOT HESITATE. I WILL READILY KILL ANYONE WHO GETS IN THE WAY. STAY QUIET AND WATCH ME.

KACHAN
...A... SURA
A...
H-HOW CAN I DO IT...?
X-XU FU?
ASURA...
HELP...
HELP!
ASURA...! NOW!
IS IT YOU, XU FU?
COME HELP ME NOW! ASURA!

XUFU!!
ASURA
SOLDIERS HAVE FOUND ME! I CANNOT SEND TELEPATHY LIKE THIS!
Ombiasa!!
PLEASE! COME AND HELP ME!
ASURA! IT'S CRITICAL HERE! COME AT ONCE!
GROAN...

AHHHHHHHH
CHICHICHIK
CHICHICHIK

CHICHICHIKCHICHICHIK
BUSHOO

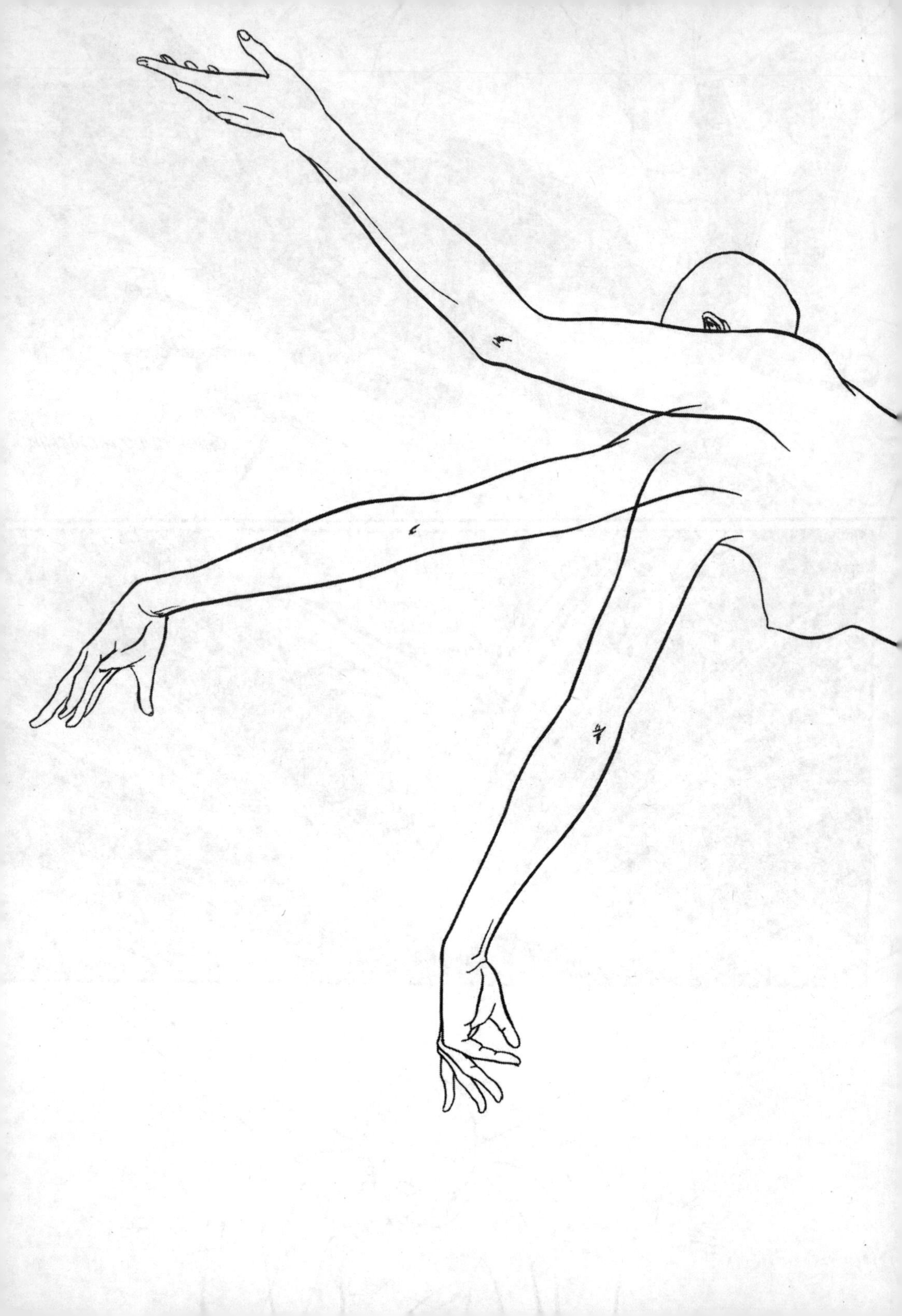

SHE HAS AWAKENED!

TAKKATAKKATAKKA
?!

SPLOOSH

STAY THERE FOR A WHILE.
ASURA! THERE ARE SOLDIERS ALL AROUND AND I CANNOT GET AWAY! HELP ME!
ASURA! THEY'VE CAUGHT ME UP! COME NOW!
XU FU! OMBIASA!
I'LL BE RIGHT THERE. HOLD ON, BOTH OF YOU!

CHAPTER 6: THE JUDGMENT

I'VE BEATEN FOUR OR FIVE, BUT... THEY SPAWN ONE AFTER ANOTHER!

POP
STOMP

!?
DAKKA
DAKKA

!
TAP
DADADAK
DAKKA
GREAT! SHOOT THE HELL OUT OF THEM!
WHACK

DAKKADAKKADAKKA
WHAM

WHY DIDN'T YOU KILL THEM?

DUNNO!

I REALLY DON'T KNOW...

THESE SOLDIERS WERE MERELY CONTROLLED BY NILA...IT'S NOT THEIR FAULT, RIGHT?

ALL LIFE FORMS ARE DIVINE, RIGHT? THEN... HUMANS ARE ALSO GODS, RIGHT?

YOU'RE SILLY. THEY'LL BE DEAD ONCE THE JUDGMENT IS DONE ANYWAY.

...HUH. ANYWAY, YOU SAVED ME. THANKS, ASURA.
NOW I CAN GIVE MY THOUGHTS FOR THE JUDGMENT.

HERE HE IS!
SHOOT TO KILL! MAKE SURE YOU GET HIM!
MEANWHILE... MADAGASCAR

DOOM

ASURA...YOU HAVE AWOKEN... WHAT A POWER! YOU SAVED ME.
THANK YOU.
I JUST WANTED TO BE OF HELP. BUT...
I'M STILL NOT SURE...IF THIS JUDGMENT IS RIGHT...

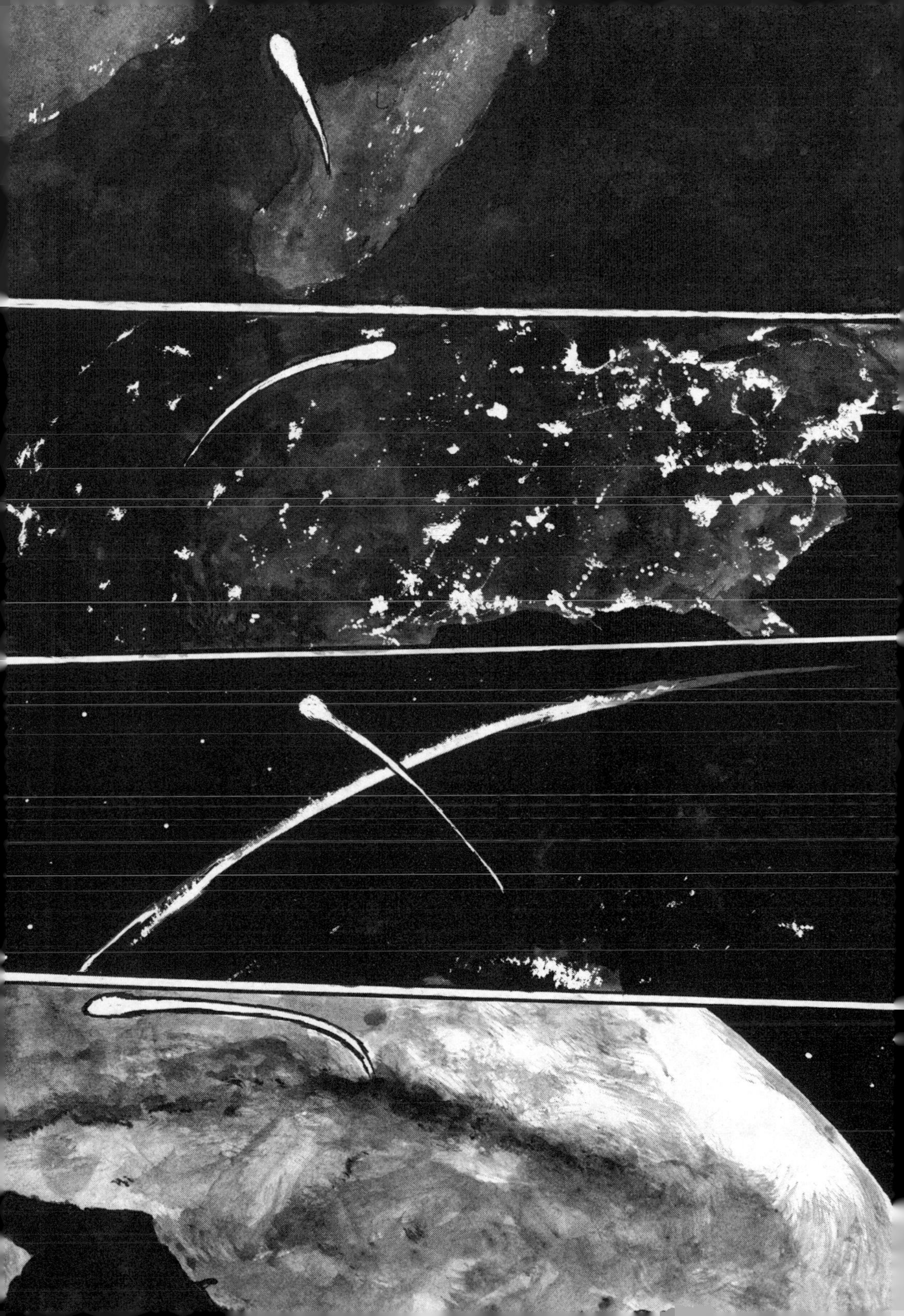

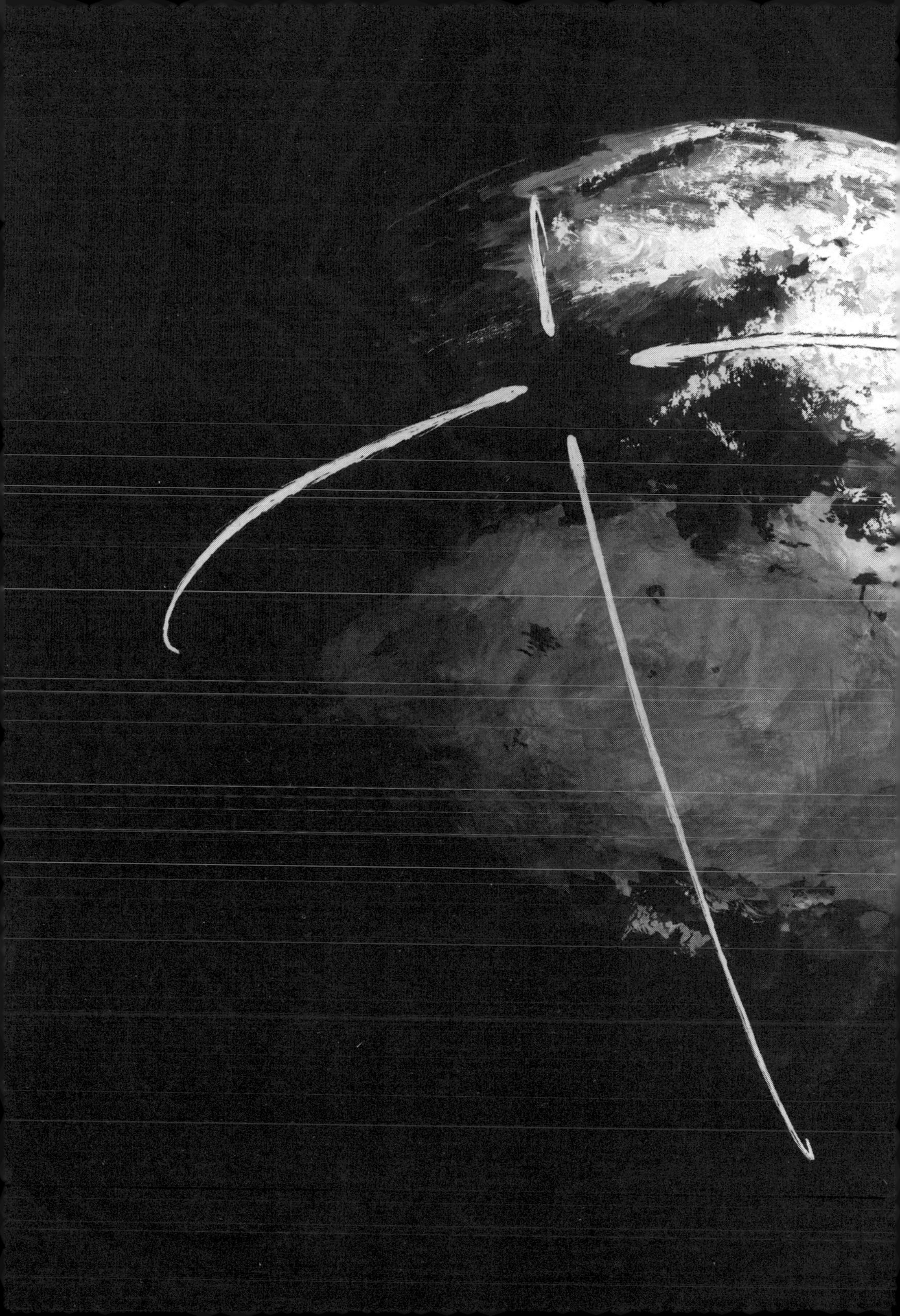

DOOM

BUSHOO

UGH!
RUMBLE RUMBLE

NILA! I WILL BANISH YOU FROM EARTH!

AS YOU WISH! I WILL KEEP LIVING!

BUT, MISTRESS PEMAJUNGNE, YOU ARE ALL FINISHED!

CHAPTER 7: METEMPSYCHOSIS

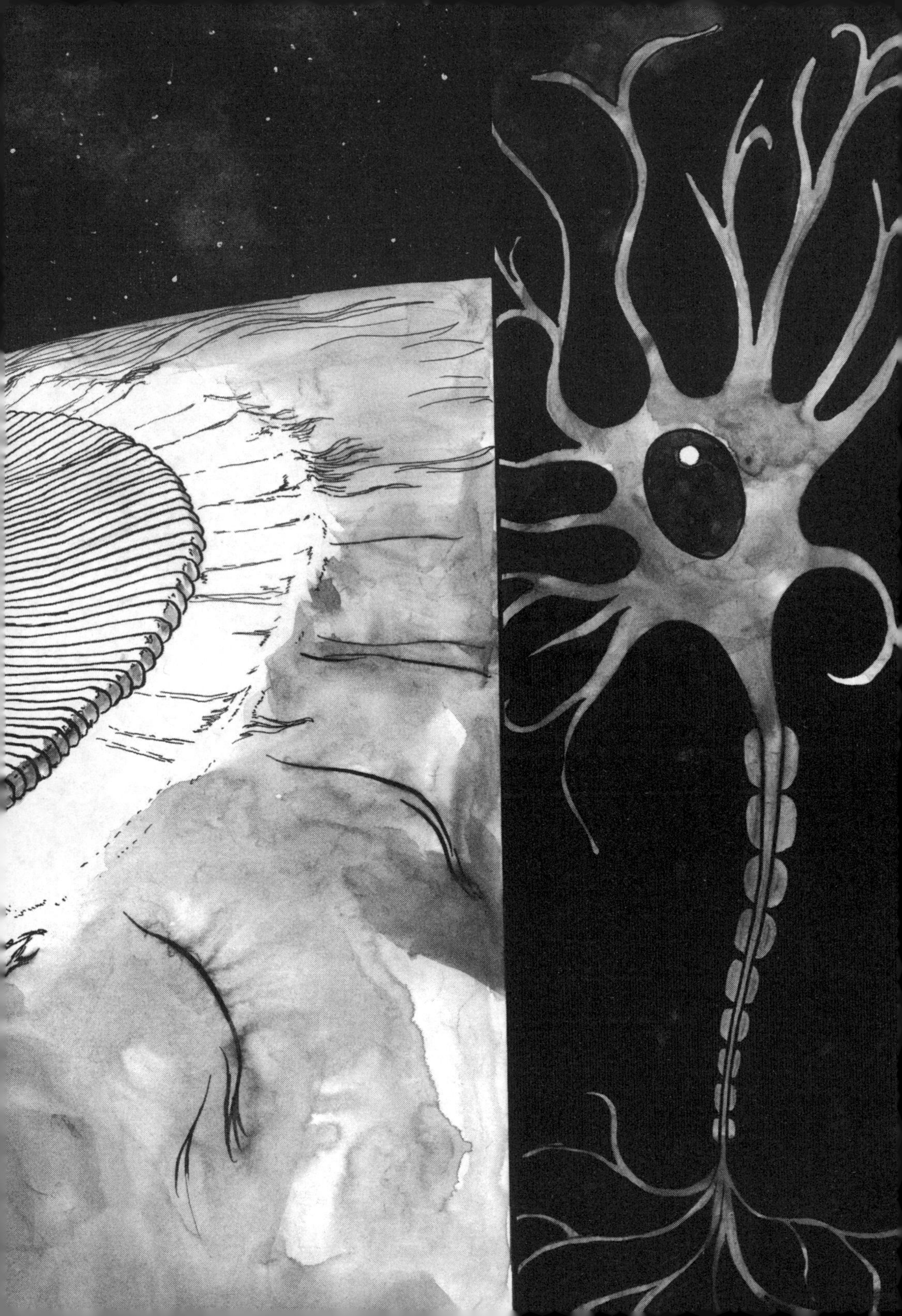

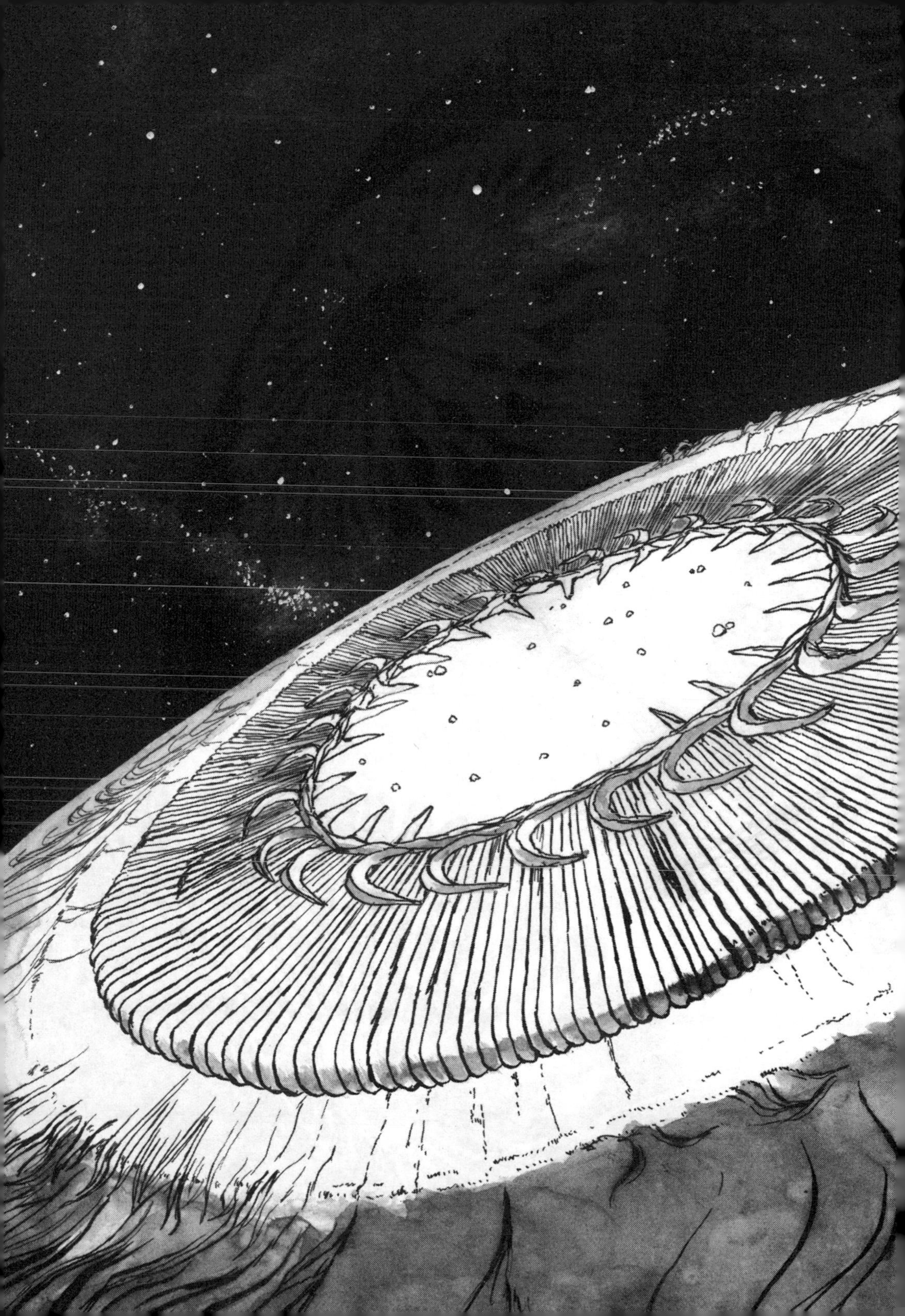

GROAN...
HONGA! WHERE ARE YOU?
HONGA!

HONGA... WHERE HAVE YOU GONE?
!!
GROAN... MY HEAD IS SPLITTING...

WHAT THE HELL IS THIS?!

I-IS IT... THE RESULT OF THE JUDGMENT?
HONGA!
THAT IS EARTH'S JUDGMENT AGAINST HUMANITY'S SINS.
EVERY SINGLE PERSON IN THE WORLD BECAME LIKE THIS? CHILDREN? BABIES, TOO?
YUP.
S-SO MERCILESS!
YOU KILLED THEM ALL?

WE DID NOT KILL THEM, ASURA.

THEY ARE NOT DEAD.

THEY ARE DEAD NO MATTER HOW YOU LOOK AT IT! DID YOU KILL ALL HUMANITY?

MISTRESS PEMAJUNGNE!

HUMANS HAVE
BEEN REINCARNATED
INTO OTHER
ORGANISMS.

SWOOOSH

SOME TURNED INTO PLANTS, OTHERS TURNED INTO ANIMALS, OR INSECTS OR MICROBES.

LIFE WILL NOT DIE.
IT CONTINUES FOREVER,
TRANSCENDING
PHYSICAL FORMS.

MISTRESS PEMAJUNGNE... NOW OUR DUTIES ARE OVER.

THAT IS RIGHT, OMBIASA.

HUH? OMBIASA! MISTRESS PEMAJUNGNE! WHAT ARE YOU TALKING ABOUT?

WHAT IS THE MATTER, ASURA?

WHAT... DO YOU MEAN THAT YOUR DUTIES ARE OVER?

SPIRITS THAT HAVE PRONOUNCED JUDGMENT HAVE COMPLETED THEIR MISSION, SO...WILL DISAPPEAR.

HUH? DISAPPEAR?

WE WILL RETURN TO THE WOMB OF THE EARTH.
HUH...?
SEE YA, ASURA.
GOOD BYE, ASURA.
LOOK AFTER YOURSELF.

XU FU! WHAT THE HELL? WHERE DID YOU GO?
HEY! OMBIASA! HONGA!
WAIT, EVERYONE!
ASURA, YOU WILL BE FINE.
NEW SPIRITS WILL APPEAR. FROM NOW ON, YOU ARE THE MISTRESS AND GUARDIAN OF EARTH.

ASURA! THIS IS XU FU. Y'ALL RIGHT? YOU MUST BE LONELY ALL BY YOURSELF.

WHAT D'YOU WANT? YOU COME AND GO AS YOU PLEASE, I SEE. AT THE END OF THE DAY, MISTRESS PEMAJUNGNE WAS THE SAME AS MISS NILA. I WAS NOTHING BUT A TOOL...

NOT SURE ABOUT THAT. MISTRESS PEMAJUNGNE CONSIDERED YOUR THOUGHTS FOR THE JUDGMENT, TOO. YOU WANTED TO SHOW MERCY TO HUMANS. THE OUTCOME WILL SOON BECOME APPARENT TO YOU. SEE YA.

ELDO YOSHIMIZU BIOGRAPHY

Born in Tokyo, Eldo Yoshimizu is an artist, sculptor, musician, and photographer.

As a sculptor, Yoshimizu creates vast, jewel-like shapes and sinuous, vivid outlines which are among Japan's most significant pieces of public art. His work has been exhibited in galleries all over the world, and he has held positions as an artist in residence in Italy, France and New York.

Yoshimizu's character of Ryuko has appeared in art galleries around Japan and Europe and has now made her jump to manga.

Teaming up with writer Benoist Simmat, his latest work is the mystifying crime thriller, *Gamma Draconis*.

THANKS

Special thanks to Mr. PATRICIO ROBLES GIL for inspiring me to draw the jungle of Madagascar.

Special thank you to Mr. VERLON JOSE for agreeing to be a model for Honga.

STOP!

This manga is presented in its original right-to-left reading format. This is the back of the book!

Pages, panels, and speech balloons read from top right to bottom left as shown above. SFX translations are placed adjacent to their original Japanese counterparts.